T his work has no pretension of being a summa about St Mary's Cathedral at Auch. Its ambition is more modest. It is simply intended to be useful. It will thus guide the steps of the friends of our Cathedral, habitual or occasional friends, to bring them to the essential.

This new edition coincides with the fifth centenary of the laying of the first stone of the Cathedral. At this occasion, the whole text has been revised, and the illustrations are now entirely in colour. Meanwhile, this work still retains the same character. We find a descriptive part. Also, since the Cathedral is the result of a common will and faith, that of the inhabitants of Auch of the period, we will not neglect, in an introduction, to put this work back into the general history of our city. However, the great originality of this work resides in everything we say about the choir stalls and the Renaissance windows of Arnaud de Moles. These two masterpieces also rightfully judged as major elements, it is fitting that we should leave them their place, or at least a priority.

These two jewels are not only art for art's sake! We shall look at them together, and above all, learn to read them. Perhaps, we can thus come to grasp, beyond the multiplicity of details, the amplitude of thought, or more precisely the soul that gives them spirit and life.

HISTORY OF THE CATHEDRAL

At the time of the Auscii

Solidly built on its headland at the top of the hill, the Cathedral of Auch naturally draws attention (pl. 1). It is impressive by its massive dimensions :

104m80 in length, 37m20 wide,
the height of its vaults is 14m and 26m
and the height of its towers is 44m.

This Cathedral is not the first at Auch. Others have preceded it on the same site. There was once a time when there was no religious edifice on this hill; for at the time, life was elsewhere. Effectively, under the Roman occupation, during the first century and at the time of the *Auscii,* a city was established and had prospered on the banks of the Gers. Auch and its inhabitants derive their name from this ancient people. The strategic importance of this city, at the crossroads of well-worn roads, and without doubt the civility of its inhabitants, merit the noble title of *Augusta Auscorum*, meaning "august city of the Auscii". In 585, after the destruction of the city of *LugdunumConvenarum* (St Bertrand-de-Comminges) by the Merovingian king Gontran, Auch became a political metropolis.

As soon as Roman tolerance allowed, a chapel dedicated to St Peter was constructed on the banks of the Gers. On this site, a parish church bore the same name. Redundant after catastrophic floods in 1977, it became a cultural centre in 1982. Later, in the 5th century, another church was built a little upstream from the first, and was dedicated to St Martin. To this day, in this place, a part of the town still carries the name of this holy Bishop of Tours.

At this same time, a priory was established near the Gers, not far from St Peter's church, a little downstream. This was the famous priory of Saint Orens, which knew a great fame and had a great influence until the Revolution.

Bishop Saint Orens, who gave the name to the priory, came to us from the Pyrenees, from St Savin, near Lourdes. Dead around 450, this Bishop has always been very honoured at Auch and in the area. St John's Church, the first Cathedral, adjoined the priory of St Orens.

Taking advantage of the decline of the Roman Empire, from the 5th century, the devastating waves of the Barbarians rose from all horizons. The Vascons coming from the north of Spain have given their name to Gascony. In such a climate of danger, from the 9th century, during the feudal period, the systematic occupation of the headland dominating the Gers to the west began. A chapel was built in the 9th century, on the arrival of Saint Taurin, Bishop of Eauze, at the See of Auch. This simple oratory, dedicated to Mary, took the place of a pagan temple, on the same rocky spur in the east-west direction. From this time, Auch became a religious metropolis, after the devastation of the town of Eauze by the Barbarians in 840.

After the year one thousand

This first chapel dedicated to Mary was replaced by a Cathedral, the second in the history of Auch. It was in Romanesque style and was the work of Saint Austinade, Archbishop in the 11th century. It construction dated from 1062, and was consecrated on 12th February 1121.

To the south-east, a canons' house in the same style adjoined this Cathedral. It had been built at the initiative of Bishop Raymond Copa, a religious, perhaps the Abbot of the Benedictines of Saint Orens. The canons' house included a cloister, various habitations, a cemetery and gardens. In this semi-monastery lived a community of priests living according to the Rule of St Augustine.

Towards this same period, an episcopal curia was established, very near this Cathedral, to the north-west.

Since the 14th century, the canons' house has been flanked, in one of its outside corners, by a tower, called the Armagnac tower. This is not to say that it belonged to the Counts of Armagnac. It depended on the canons' house and the Archbishops of Auch. Over the centuries, the canons' house fell into spiritual and material decadence. Restored and rearranged at the end of the 19th century, it is now used as a sacristy and outbuildings. In its basement, one can see the last vestiges, essentially the remains of a chapter house in brick. Gemeled pillars bear capitals decorated with pine-cones. On the vault, the frescos in poor condition have suffered from the humidity. In 1988, they were removed and restored, with the intention of placing them in a better place.

The Monuments Historiques have a project, already being realised, in view to renovation of these basements. The chapter house, at present partially destroyed and even divided into compartments, will find its unity again. It will even be used, with an entry from the outside, from the Place Salinis. From then, the remaining pillars and capitals will be open to visits. For the other parts of these basements, also restored, they will continue to be used by the parish.

Adjoining the Cathedral at the south is the Place Salinis, with plants and a fountain in the middle, dates from 1860. On the east side, a monumental staircase of 232 steps allows direct access from the lower town. In the abrupt part, to the south of this place, there are steep narrow streets, called pousterles (small doors). They evoke the fifteenth century town.

Concerning the episcopal curia adjoining the Cathedral from the 11th century, this was enlarged and embellished in the 18th century under the episcopate of Bishop de Montillet. This grandiose construction, in pure classical style, was transformed into the prefecture at the beginning of the 20th century.

Construction of the Gothic Cathedral

Bad weather, wars between lords and other responsible authorities, won over the Romanesque Cathedral of Saint Austinade, as for the provisional edifices replacing it. Then another Cathedral was thought of, to be more beautiful and bigger. This project, envisaged for a long time, matured under the episcopates of Jean de Lescun (1463-1483) and François Philibert de Savoie (1483-1490). This ambitious enterprise was entrusted to a famous monk Jean Marre, to whom we owe notably the Cathedral of Condom. This monk architect designed a grandiose plan, to be realised progressively. This was to be a Gothic Cathedral with three aisles, with a particularly developed apse. Naturally, the stress on the diagonal ribs would be neutralised at the level of the lower aisles by buttresses, and at the level of the high aisles by flying buttresses resting on these buttresses. However, it was practically impossible to extend to the north of the Cathedral. To the west, where the present square is located, this area was not finally cleared until under the supervision of Etigny (1753-1767). It was thus necessary, to the south, to encroach on the canons' house, and to the east, gain on an abrupt slope. This last difficulty was resolved by the elevation of a supporting crypt on the rock of the hill. This was much better than the solution of bringing earth. The outside part of the apse therefore rests on this most solid foundation. The foundation stone of the new Cathedral was very solemnly laid on 4th July 1489. The work accelerated. On 12th February 1548, it was possible to go ahead with the ceremonies of consecration. An inscription, perfectly legible on one of the pillars of the choir, reminds us of this date. The major elements being finished in the apse, more particularly the ambulatory chapels and the vaults covering them, and above all the 18 windows of Arnaud de Moles and the 113 stalls. However, the central vault was not up. This did not prevent offices from being sung in choir, from before 1548. A provisional ceiling and roof gave shelter in awaiting the definitive vault, protected by a wall to the west at the level of the transept.

On the other hand, in the transepts and aisles, in 1548, everything was only in the early stages. We owe especially the three western porches and the bell towers up to the height of the lower aisles to the architect Jean de Beaujeu (1560-1567). The four spiral staircases, in stone, at the two extremities of the transept, to get to the triforiums, were installed towards 1635. One of them, situated in the so-called limaçon staircase, is particularly original. Its central core is empty, and one can have the impression that the steps are ordered around a pivot of air.

On his arrival at Auch, in 1629, Archbishop Dominique de Vic gave a new thrust to the construction of the Cathedral, almost at a standstill since 1548, notably in the aisles, partly due to the fact of the mortgage represented by the cemetery situated in that place. The work therefore accelerated, to such a point that the building work was practically finished inside at the death of this prelate in 1661.

In 1672, the architects Pierre Mercier and Pierre Miressus took on the building of the towers, the two final storeys. Their sculpted decor, finished in 1680, is the work of François Auxion. The two towers are occupied by a peal of nine bells. Eight are in the north tower. The clock tower contains the heaviest of them: the great bell weighing 9700 kilos.

Variety of styles

Thus, since the laying of the foundation stone in 1489, to the carved decoration of the west front in 1680, nearly 200 years elapsed. Despite this, we find inside a real architectural unity (pl. 3). The ribbing was chosen, the vault over crossed ribs, in Gothic style. This choice was retained regardless. Meanwhile, tastes had evolved and so had fashions. Successive architects did not fear to take inspiration sometimes. At the same time, they were careful not to break the harmony of this fine ensemble. The Gothic style had now become flamboyant. In some places, it had given place to the Renaissance style. We find this more particularly in the minor architecture and the secondary decorations: the windows of Arnaud de Moles, the choir stalls, the stained glass and the rose window of the 17th century, the retables, chapel credences, triforiums, etc.

At the level of the lofts, in the walls of the high aisles, there are the triforiums under basket-handle arches. This resembles Renaissance style balconies. Doors give access. Originally, according to their first design, these triforiums were a continuous corridor, a kind of gallery running the whole length of the vaults and inside the lofts to give daylight. In the concrete case of our Cathedral, they appear like a superfluous decoration without practical use.

The two doors of the north and south of the transept, the three western porches, the carved decoration of the two towers are clearly of the Renaissance (pl. 2). We see there arches, pediments, a whole series of friezes and bas-reliefs, many niches to receive statues. Columns and Corinthian style pilasters support entablatures crowned by balustrades.

Furnishing

The furnishing of the Cathedral was made progressively, as the construction of the edifice advanced. The apse was the first to be furnished before 1548 especially with altars for a few of the chapels. There remains from this time a Renaissance altar dating from 1524 in chapel 15; the very beautiful baldachino, ornamented with open-work and carved, in the axial chapel (retro-choir); the remarkable Burial of Christ in chapel 17.

In 1609, the architect Pierre Souffron II began to erect the monumental decoration that closes the eastern semi-cycle from the choir. Meanwhile, the interior furnishing of the Cathedral was not truly decided upon until 1648, when all the vaults and windows were installed. In 1671, the sculptor Gervais Drouet was charged with the installation of a choir screen, adjoining the west side of the stalls, in the transept. He was asked to close the chapels with a balustrade in marble. But, a few years sooner, in 1662, another sculptor, Jean Douillé, had received an order for 13 retables: 10 for the aisles and 3 pour the apse chapels that were not yet furnished. These retables were to be in gilded or polychrome wood. On their surface, and sometimes at two levels, an episode of the life of Christ, of Our Lady or a Saint was represented in bas-relief, inspired by the name of the chapel. Among the 13 retables of Jean Douillé, only 3 have survived to our own days, two entirely intact in chapels 10 and 19, the other partially in chapel 7.

The chapels and their dedication

The Cathedral contains a set of 21 chapels: 10 in the nave aisles and 11 in the apse. In the 17th century, when Jean Douillé took on his important work, the 10 nave chapels were dedicated to Our Lady. For each of them, the event corresponding with the dedication was represented by a sculpture in bas-relief in the central part of the retable. Alas, most of these monuments have disappeared. Meanwhile, in their ensemble, these 10 chapels have remained despite all under the name of Our Lady. The events of her life, chosen from among the most essential, are chronologically ordered. To get to know them and to meditate upon them, it suffices to see the nave chapels successively from the left towards the right, going from the main entry.

On the other hand, in the apse chapels, the dedications to Christ are numerous. They competed against dedications to the Saints: St Martial and St James, very popular in our area, St Anne and St Catherine. As in the nave aisles, a visit of the apse chapels must be made from the left to the right from the transept. It is the cycle of the Saints that comes first, then, from the axial chapel (retro-choir), the cycle of Christ's life. However, both develop by following a same progression: a pilgrimage, not without suffering, towards the perfect joy of the Resurrection.

An even more Marian Cathedral

In the 18th century, popular devotion to Our Lady began to invade the sanctuary itself, the apse. She seems to have taken possession of a few of the chapels, a total of five, now dedicated to her. In these chapels, episodes of her life are not evoked as in the nave chapels, but simply one or another of the mysteries that most marked her soul, or her holiness.

This evolution for the choice of titles and dedications in the chapels, is characteristic of a period and above all of a certain faith. It is a faith that tends to become increasingly Marian, but in the most overall sense, in the most integral meaning of the word, according to the ancient maxim: to Jesus through Mary. This means that it is in the person of Mary, the Mother of God, that the Son is also worshipped; and through Him, all the values He represents. This is how believers understood their faith during this period. We find written testimony in one of the choir stalls (n° 25). This writing, which is therefore a sculpture, reproduces textually, for us, one of the refrains of the 16th century in these terms:

Who puts his heart with the Mother of God,
He has his heart and he has God.
And he who puts it in another God,
He loses his heart and he loses God...

The Black Virgin

These two words, suggesting initiation, hide a spiritual reality, very much alive, over the whole length of our humanity. She is a hidden presence bringing the faithful soul, possibly a pilgrim, to his destination, in view to a spiritual rebirth.

The Black Virgin is that of Chartres among others. Her colour, black, is the colour of night; the night for the birth of a new day. This Cathedral is dedicated to her. The inscription is engraved in black marble, in the porch, over the central door, translated from Latin: To Mary, the Virgin who is to give birth to God.

We have at least two representations of the Black Virgin in the Cathedral. Her personality is not expressly materialised in this black colour, but clearly suggested by very circumstantial details. One of these representation is found in one of the apse windows, in chapel 13, under the cover of the sibyl of Samos. Her costume, as her face, are in dark brown, marking the background colour of this window. Above all, this sibyl, with a cradle in her hand, finds herself expecting maternity. The inscription, on the base of the character, carries the name Sanne, which can be read as St Anne, one of the two figures, drawn precisely, of the Black Virgin; the other being the Virgin Mary. Mary figures in the lower playlet, representing the Nativity of Jesus. The child, who was to come, is born; and Mary, keeping Him company, has become Virgin of Light.

The other character, figuring the Black Virgin, is found in the choir stalls, in the canopies, immediately after the panel representing Adam and Eve. It is named Charity. This word is very clearly written on the phylactery she holds in both hands. The two children, as small as dwarfs and standing at her feet, are waiting and stretching their hands towards her. The child called hope is to be born of this woman.

VISIT OF THE NAVE CHAPELS

The visit of these chapels is made from the left to the right, going from the main entrance (see plan p. 10).

1) Chapel of the Immaculate Conception

Retable in stone of the 19th century. In the lower part, a painting signed by Lagarde represents the Virgin of the Apocalypse.

The Baptismal Font, in black marble, is the work of Lacroix (1675).

2) Chapel of St Theresa

The retable, installed in this chapel since the Revolution, comes from the old Carmelite nunnery that became a public library. It dates from the 17th century. It is a fine ensemble, discreet and sober, according to Carmelite spirituality. A recent restoration gave back its beauty in 1970.

The two statues, on each side of the central piece, represent St Theresa of Avila and St John of the Cross, the reformers of the Carmelite Order. The painting commemorates the giving of the Scapular to St Simon Stock and St Magdalene of Pazzi in prayer.

In this chapel was found a very fine painting of the intendant of Pomereu, deceased in 1734. This monument, mutilated during the Revolution, was restored in 1950. It can be seen in Auch city museum.

On the floor, a simple stone bears the inscription of this deceased person. On the north wall is attached a memorial, in relation with this event. At the top, a medallion; lower down, a weeping woman symbolising the mourning of the whole of Gascony. The shield bears the arms of Béarn and the city of Auch.

3) Chapel of the Presentation

Retable in stone of the 19th century. The dedication is painted in the top painting. Lower down, another painting represents the meeting of Jesus and St John the Baptist.

On the floor, burial of P. Molière, his wife and relations (1692).

Plan of the nave and apse

4) Chapel of St Joseph

Retable in stone of the 19th century. At the top, the statue of the Saint. At the bottom, a painting signed by Lagarde, a local artiste. Dated from 1805, it evokes the marriage of St Joseph.

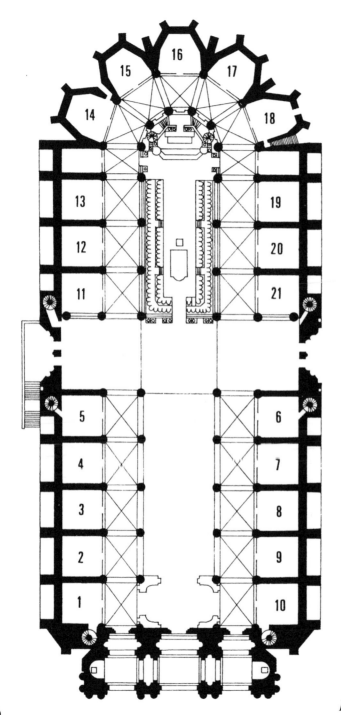

Plan of the nave and apse

On the floor, burial of Mgr Virgile Joseph Béguin, Bishop of Auch (1935-1955) who died in 1955.

5) Chapel of the Annunciation

Retable of the 19th century in stone. A bas-relief represents the dedication. It is the work of Ferri, an Italian artist, living at Auch.

On a pedestal is enthroned a statue of the 18th century, in gilded wood; venerated as Our Lady of Auch. She is dressed in the fashion of Spanish Virgins.

6) Chapel of St John the Baptist

Retable of the 18th century in stone. There are twisted spiral columns with vine branches rolled around them. The statue of the Saint is at the top with his symbols: the standard and the lamb. At the bottom, St Vincent de Paul appears on the clouds.

7) Chapel of the Nativity

The central panel of this retable, in gilded wood, is from the 17th century. It is the work of Jean Douillé.

St Eloi is at the top with the hammer on the anvil at his feet. He is the Patron Saint of blacksmiths and associated trades working in wood, iron or stone. The theme of St Eloi's hammer is very widely evoked in the choir stalls and the windows of Arnaud de Moles.

There is a Renaissance credence at the south wall. In the retable, the Nativity (pl. 4), in bas-relief, deserves prolonged attention, for it is typical of the art of the period. It is presented as a naive work, which cares little for proportions, ignoring the rules of perspective. This ensemble is very well ordered. The characters expressing joy, in admiration, are grouped in concentric circles around the Infant Jesus at the centre. The most important are the nearest; and as is expected, the Angels are found at the top of the panel. Among these characters, we notice embryos of capitals and pilasters. They evoke a timid quest for perspective. The bound lamb, resting at the foot of the crib, is not without relation with the Jesus of the Nativity of Arnaud de Moles (chapel 13). Jesus appears Himself as bound, and ready for the Sacrifice.

8) *Chapel of the Purification*

19th century stone retable.

Painting of the Presentation of Jesus at the Temple. In the extreme corners and in the background, there are two statues in niches: St Joseph to the right and St Augustine to the left.

On the floor, the tomb of Louis Daignon de Sendat, Vicar General of the Diocese. He collected many manuscripts and founded the public library. He died in 1764.

There is a Renaissance credence at the south wall.

9) *Chapel of Our Lady of the Agonising*

This chapel is now dedicated to St Anthony, from when it received the tomb of Antoine de Mégret d'Etigny, intendant of the generality of Auch. This tomb was formerly in the old priory church of Saint Orens. Carved by the sculptor Lucas from Toulouse, it was demolished during the Revolution. A reproduction from 1803 has been placed in this chapel. The model is kept at the Museum of Auch.

On the floor, a slab evokes this death of 1767. The memorial tomb is in the wall. Bas-reliefs symbolise, under a medallion, the mourning of his wife and the town.

The retable of this chapel was installed in 1860, under the episcopate of Salinis. This ensemble is made of scattered elements, columns and capitals in red marble, coming from the former choir screen, which was the work of Gervais Drouet in 1761. Between the columns is found the statue of St Anthony the Hermit.

10) *Chapel of the Assumption*

This retable in polychrome and gilded wood dates from 1662. We owe it to the sculptor Jean Douillé. The dedication of this chapel is evoked in two panels in bas-relief. The lower one represents the Dormition of the Virgin. The Apostles and disciples, 15 of them, are grouped around an empty tomb, where the body of Mary had been laid. They meditate on the mystery of the Assumption, which is sculpted at the top. We see Angels taking the body of Mary to heaven.

This retable, one of the most beautiful of the Cathedral, was restored in 1964. The ornamentation is rich and the polychrome is discreet and delicate.

The Crossing and "Front Choir"

From 1671, a monumental choir screen was erected at the western part of the choir stalls. This work of Gervais Drouet is presented as a vast ensemble of Corinthian columns in red marble. At the top were placed separated statues ordered as in a Calvary: the Cross, Mary and St John, the two Prophets David and Isaiah. Half way up, above the central door, the four Evangelists sit around a table. At the beginning of the 19th century, two altars had been built against this choir screen, each side of the door. The north altar, dedicated to Mary, was used for parish Masses. That of the south was dedicated to St Roch.

In 1860, Bishop de Salinis decided to arrange the crossing. It took the name of "front choir". It includes a painted decoration, stalls to the north and south and an altar in the middle. The altar is in sculpted white stone. Bas-reliefs represent a few events of the life of Our Lady, Patron Saint of Auch. At the east, the painted decoration is the work of the Parisian artist A. Dauvergne. On a background of gold, we see the four Evangelists alternating with the four great Prophets. Under the organ gallery, a Virgin and Child are surrounded by Angels honouring them. This painted ensemble, peopled by Saints, reminds us of the famous iconostases of oriental churches. A choir organ, in Romantic style, crowns the whole.

Elements of Gervais Drouet's choir screen are scattered around the Cathedral. The statues have been transferred to the vast platform of the choir retable. The Corinthian columns enter the composition of the two retables of chapels 9 and 21. But everything, created by Archbishop Antoine de Salinis, has been reordered in 1970. The stalls were moved further apart and placed in line with the pillars. The retable was removed from the altar for Mass facing the people, and the altar is at the centre of the crossing. Our Lady of Auch, who dominated this altar for some time, was placed in the chapel of the Annunciation.

The Pulpit

The very fine pulpit, in gilded wood, which can be seen attached to a pillar of the nave, is owed to Archbishop Jean de Montillet (1742-1776). It is in the style of the 18th century.

The gates in wrought iron, closing the three western porches, date from the same period. They bear the arms of this Archbishop.

We have made a first visit, with the two stages it involves: the three aisles and then the "forward choir" in the crossing of the transepts. Of course, we have looked at the various beauties available to us.

However, there is another way of looking at things that is strongly advised, in relational life and also in the domain of art. This is in view to access to a certain vision, not at all obvious to a first view, but what can be of benefit to us.

Our religious edifices and their masterpieces have each their vision, in a moral and spiritual meaning. We are going to contemplate the Renaissance windows and the choir stalls during this third and final stage of this visit.

GLIMPSE OF THE TECHNIQUES OF STAINED GLASS

For stained glass, the ideal proportion is broken down into 1/3 silicon and 2/3 charred soda. Habitually, river sand provides the silicon, the ashes of beech and bracken give the charred soda, and a calcium stabilising agent was added. This is why glass workshops were normally established not far from a river and near a forest, for a great quantity of timber was necessary for the vitrification of the silicon.

After firing, the still liquid glass was reduced to plates by one or another of the usual techniques, of which the essential element was blowing. By blowing, the volume of a gooey mass of glass was augmented, under the action of weight or according to the movement of centrifugal force. The most practised technique consisted of firstly obtaining a hollow ball, then a relatively long cylinder, by blowing into a kind of hollow iron cane. At the end of this operation, the cylinder was cut at both ends, then cut along its length, before being laid on a flat support.

To obtain glass coloured in its mass, it sufficed to add alloys of powders during fusion. Glass coloured in its mass was distinguished from plated glass. Plating as practised from the 12th century consisted in re-firing plain glass with a superimposed coat of coloured glass. The red colour was used only by plating.

In France of the 16th century, one learnt to engrave the plating with abrasives, under the action of a steel cutting wheel mounted on a lathe. This enabled the worker to bring out motives, for example, an inscription on white glass by scratching the coloured plating. They also practised the art of inserted glass, within and over the whole thickness of another piece of plain or coloured glass. In the series of 18 windows of Arnaud de

Moles, we find several examples of inset or engraved glass, particularly in chapels 12, 13 and 14.

To reduce the glass to a drawn form, it was cut with a red-hot iron. In each piece cut out, the drawing has been traced in grisaille, which was one of the first colours to paint. It was with grisaille that shadows, lines of faces and folds of garments were given. Later, in the 13th century, silver yellow and then other colours appeared: sepia, rust brown, green and above all blood red. Silver yellow was essentially used to translate orna-mentation motives, blood red gave a rosy hue that was very near to natu-ral flesh.

Even dry, the grisaille and other painted colours do not adhere solidly to glass. They must imperatively be fixed by firing. Then only the various pieces of glass are ready to be fixed to each other with double-grooved pieces of lead. When everything is assembled, the pane is placed in the corresponding window.

THE 62 WINDOWS

Progressive installation

For the Feast of the Dedication, on 12th February 1548, only the lower choir windows had their stained glass. They were installed by Arnaud de Moles, a master glazier of Saint-Sever, in the Gascony Landes. The signa-ture and date (1513) are read in the last window of this remarkable series.

But, it is only a hundred years later that the other windows began to be installed in their turn as the construction of the edifice advanced.

(continued on p. 33)

PLATES

RENAISSANCE ARCHITECTURE, FURNISHINGS AND WINDOWS

(continued on p. 48)

1

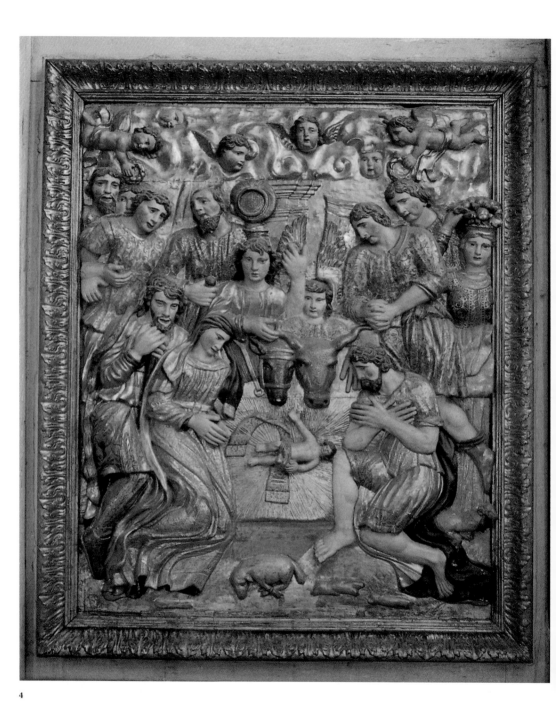

6

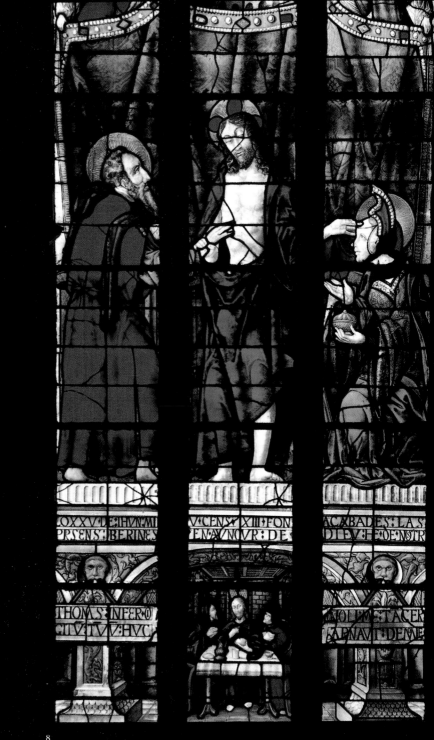

11

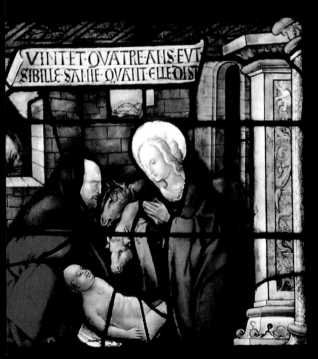

VINT ET OVATRE AIIS EVT
SIBILLE SAMIE QVAIT ELLE DIST

12

17

In 1620, the high windows of the choir at last received their glass. They are the work of François Bierges, glazier of Auch, and Pierre Autipout, glazier of Gimont. Some years later, in 1641, this same Pierre Autipout installed the glass of the high windows of the nave and three rose windows. The two transept rose windows are dedicated to Saints Peter and Paul. The third, that of the west end, pays homage to Mary. The low windows of the nave were the last to be installed by a Flemish glazier, James Damen, who carried out this task in 1648.

Variety of styles

In all the windows, placed after 1620, we find the same characteristics, even through the authors were different. Apparently, they are not truly painted glass, like those of Arnaud de Moles, but plain glass. Tastes have without doubt changed.

Also, it is possible that more light was desired inside the edifice. Then, new sets with characters in the style of the old windows signed in 1513 would have seemed superfluous, or at least a pale reflection. But, above all, after the Council of Trent (1563), the Roman authorities had resisted the use of images in churches, to remedy excesses, and mainly because the inspiration tended to become secular.

The monotony of the plain glass is broken, very discreetly, by vertical bands going up the border of the lancets. Filling up the mullions and the surface of these vertical bands, the decoration seems very ordered. It consists of a series of miniature designs: birds, fruit, vases of flowers, leaves, many medallions with human faces, monograms of Mary and Christ.

THE WINDOWS OF ARNAUD DE MOLES

Interest of this set

It is above all the windows of Arnaud de Moles that deserve our attention. Produced between 1507 and 1513, they are esteemed as the finest of the Renaissance. Also, this reputation is not usurped. Emile Male, the very appreciated art critic recognises: "For the breadth of thought, no work of this period equals the windows of Auch".

They occupy all the windows, in the ambulatory chapels. Only one is without stained glass, that of the Holy Sepulchre, through impossibility, for it was hard against the wall of the old Bishop's curia. The visit of these windows must be made as for the apse chapels, from the left to the right going from the transept. You need to begin with chapel 11.

The clarity of a story

This extraordinary set includes a series of 18 windows. They are presented as a rich decoration, where a crowd of characters of every origin meets each other. Most come from the Bible. But some of them, like the sibyls, are borrowed from pagan religions. Meanwhile, not everything is mixed willy-nilly. We find a relatively precise ordering, and a certain symmetry to begin with, in the highlighted windows with a story. These windows, three of them, are said to tell a story, because a fact from the Bible is clearly narrated. Thus, it is not necessary to make a prior decoding to guess the secret. The themes of these three story windows have been chosen with the greatest care. They evoke important truths that will inspire and clarify the whole of the story that develops from chapel to chapel.

These three have received a place of choice. They are situated in the most crucial points, at the most decisive points of intersection. The first was placed at the beginning, at the cradle of all things, for good or evil. It evokes the first origins: the Creation and Original Sin. The second, which represents the crucifixion of Jesus, has it just place in the retro-choir. He presides at the most important point of the semi-circle. He appears as the pivot where the destiny of history is definitively oriented, for good or evil. Finally, the third has its place at the end of the cycle, where it evokes salvation offered in the Risen Christ. It is the crowning, the perfect fulfilment of the whole work.

The enigma of a story

The other windows, fifteen of them, are presented differently. The ordering is not the same. We no longer see coherent sets, but characters that seem to ignore each other. The ideas and themes are unclear. The message is not read immediately, but rather in a far perspective, beyond what is visible. To discover it, we need to make a difficult decoding, that is to find the golden thread creating an invisible link between heterogeneous characters, apparently strangers to each other.

An idea brings them together. Which one? The key to this mystery is in the hands of the sibyl. The object she carries gives us the key to the enigma. This symbolic biblical object concerns each of the characters in a same window in some way. It brings them together for a single idea. The artist provoked these encounters, to clarify a theme, to illustrate a story.

Ordering of the characters

At the same time, we remark some ordering, even in these windows without a story. This is not without interest, even if this does not teach us anything essential. To begin with, a certain alternation regularly renews itself. We find ourselves still in a same window, a Patriarch, a Prophet, and Apostle and a sibyl. When a chapel contains three windows, this happens three times, there is generally only one sibyl in this case. However, the Patriarchs, Prophets and Apostles always accompany her, in a more or less equal number.

Similarly to these regular alternations, we find another and more rigorous and essential ordering. It emphasises the stages of historical progress. It is a question of Patriarchs like Noah, Abraham, Isaac, etc., distributed in the chapels according to chronological order.

Serving a story

These windows are not a gallery of merely famous characters. Among the most illustrious, some of them are not there, but some lesser known characters occupy a place of choice. What counts first of all is not the character itself but the story it evokes, the destiny it attempts to direct. Like the sibyls, each is dedicated to serving a story. They find themselves at the heart, the very crucible. They come from everywhere, they are from all classes, from every origin. They come willingly like celebrity artists, finding themselves in gigantic galas, not for their own benefit, but to the contrary to the advantage of a social and humanitarian task. These celebrity characters of Arnaud de Moles' windows also come from everywhere, most from the Bible, some from Paganism. They contribute, in their own way, to the illustration of the greatest epic, nothing other than the unique testimony of the LOVE OF GOD, Creator and Father, in the unfolding of a HISTORY, in the intimacy of each story. Such was the profound desire of the artist. Before signing his work, he insisted on writing the very meaningful dedication: *To the glory of* God and Our Lady.

Art of stained glass : a long evolution

The word window would fit better the whole set of our windows, especially those of Arnaud de Moles. They occupy a maximum of wall surface. Above all, the decoration becomes predominant to such a point that it seems to prevail over colour. During the golden age of stained glass, this was not the case. Then, the balance between colour and design was perfect. A harmony resting and filling the view, all in giving full satisfaction to the spirit. The windows of Chartres are a model in this domain.

It is only progressively that such perfection was achieved. It was necessary to experiment for a long time. In the beginning, all glass was plain and the windows of an extreme simplicity. The surface of these windows began to be organised from the inside, more particularly in the disposition of the leading linking the panes together. This was in the 9th century. The infinite variety of geometrical designs allows original compositions. Then, colour started to be introduced into the mass of the glass. The diversity of colours, associated with the variety of design, enables the artist to attain a certain beauty that harmonises well with the lines of interior architecture that itself attempted a similar effort.

However, very soon, the art of stained glass knew another evolution. As a new world, that of humanism, for time advanced towards the Renaissance. We now see an invasion by design, that of statues with various monumental decorations coming to occupy all the space. Until then, the window remained a flat surface. Now, perspective is introduced and remains, first through appearances of niches, then by reproductions of decorations, borrowed from various styles, by the relief attempting to give expression to faces and very ample folds in garments, finally by the landscape backgrounds further and further away. At the end of this evolution, most of these creations, inspired by the renewed art, are no longer stained glass windows in the strict meaning of the words, but painted glass. The master glaziers gave way to painter-decorators.

A will to serve

In a certain way, for glaziers or stained glass, it is the same thing in a film, at the cinema or on television. We find a screenplay, choreography, a decor and sometimes background music. It is a lengthily thought-out programme. It is the same thing for our Renaissance windows. It is also a kind of "screenplay", with the succession of various mainly biblical themes, where a very strong thought is expressed. There is also a whole decor, with historic perspectives, one of the marks of this period when this masterpiece was realised. As for the so-called "background music", it is the reflection of a culture, a certain human sensitivity, that of our Renaissance Europe.

Now, a question is asked! What was the real role of Arnaud de Moles, the master glazier, in the realisation of this opus that bears his signature? He did not have absolute control, as in the case of a choreographer, a decorator, a photographer or a musician in a cinema production. It is therefore by several artists, but always in the most perfect complementarity that we finally arrived at this realisation.

Therefore, Arnaud de Moles played his role, but only his role. Meanwhile, he had in himself all the necessary abilities in view to making a perfect synthesis, from very precise points given to him: biblical and historical points for precise events and characters of this period.

A great artistic adaptability

At the end of the day, Arnaud de Moles showed himself truly as a master for the realisation of the kind of "screenplay" entrusted to him, but also in his own responsibilities as a painter-decorator. A clever workman formed at the school of the Compagnons, he was able to make of himself a school. His school was not frankly of the Renaissance, but still marked by the techniques of the Middle Ages and the Gothic period. This is what comes out of his work in general, of which there remain a few vestiges in our Gascony.

At the same time, this artist was a man of his time, therefore himself of the humanist spirit. He did not ignore the Renaissance, and he even adhered to it assiduously. He was of great sensitivity, and consequently was perfectly able to be at one with the various patrons who called upon him. His companions as glass painters were like him, earnest, available and applied to their task.

Therefore, his work is marked by his personality. Among other things, we find his originality of colours and the permanence of a certain optimism. This optimism shows itself clearly in the biblical themes entrusted to him. He knew how to interpret them well to transmit their serene joy to us, in the decors, through the expression of characters and with colours of a very evocative compatibility.

Concerning the colours, they are of very characteristic shades: red, blue, green, old gold, amethyst violet, crimson red, etc., colours that appear living and warm under intense light, becoming profound and mystical in a more diffused light. Arnaud de Mole was a past-master in the art of giving nuances, by a damask effect, in the costumes as in the decors.

Narrative of a story

The 18 windows of Arnaud de Moles are therefore an exceptional piece of work. What remains truly unique, in this ensemble like in the choir stalls, is the message that comes out. Arnaud de Moles was not the inspiration. He did not have this genius. This thought was given by unknown patrons, without doubt by the Archbishop of Clermont-Lodève, who held the See of Auch from 1507. At that time, none of the lower windows of the choir had stained glass. This Cardinal-Archbishop was concerned. For the themes to be represented, he was inspired by the general humanism of the Italian Renaissance. This humanism was giving a new dimension to the great biblical epic. This particularly marked the work of Michelangelo, especially his famous frescos on the vault of the Sistine Chapel at Rome.

We find these same flights at Auch, in the choir woodwork, on the windows of Arnaud de Moles. It is a question of HISTORY, that of the Hebrews. It is told as the visit is made. It advances and develops at the rhythm of life and the seasons. However, this history is not simple. It is even very complex, since, in parallel, it already prefigures the life of Christ and the future of the Church, the new People of God charged with continuing His work.

In the windows of Arnaud de Moles, the history of the Hebrews is told in the central part, where the great characters are found. The life of Christ is evoked in the playlets occupying the lower part. As a general rule, these little panels are in more or less close relation with the corresponding great characters.

APSE CHAPELS

The visit of these chapels is made from the left to the right, going from the transept (see schematic plan p. 10).

11) Purgatory Chapel

Graced with six Corinthian columns in red marble, this 17th century stone retable appears as a replica of the old choir screen: same architecture, same materials. Could it be by Gervais Drouet? This wall had previously been decorated with frescos. There is a painting in the lower part of the retable signed by Lagarde representing Purgatory.

On the north wall, a small funerary monument encloses the heart of Mgr de la Croix d'Azolette, Archbishop of Auch (1840-1856) who died at Lyons in 1861.

We find on the floor the resting places of three Archbishops of Auch: Mgr d'Apchon (1775-1783), Mgr Balain (1890-1905) and Mgr Ricard (1907-1935) who died in 1944.

WINDOW OF ARNAUD DE MOLES (n° 1)

General theme : the six days of Creation and the seventh day. Alas! With Original Sin, evil entered the world. Meanwhile, the Redemption is announced : the Day of the Lord will come.

At the top, under the arch on the rib : God presides over the birth of the world, over the creation of Adam and Eve (pl. 6). *Characters at the foot* : Adam and Eve by the tree of the forbidden fruit. I*n the lower part* : Adam and Eve chased away from Paradise, then to work; Cain kills Abel.

12) Chapel of the Holy Heart of Mary

Six columns of black marble grace this stone retable of the 17th century. St Martial was patron of this chapel until the 18th century. The present dedication is represented in a painting *to the bottom. At the top,* we notice the statue of St Margaret of Antioch, who figured as the Goddess Reason during the Revolution.

We find on the floor the resting place of Mgr Maurice Rigaud, Archbishop of Auch who died on 29th December 1984.

WINDOW OF ARNAUD DE MOLES (n° 2)

General theme : we see successive and progressive beginnings, notably on a religious level. Hope is brought by the palm in the sibyl's hands.

In the mullions, God the Creator, in the middle of the choir of Angels. *Characters at the foot* : Noah, Ezekiel, St Peter the Apostle, the sibyl of Eythrea (pl. 9). *At the bottom* : drunkenness of Noah, blessing of Jacob (the Israel of God), St Peter the Apostle walks on water, finally the Annunciation.

Above Noah, on the stand are painted the arms of the Cardinal Archbishop Clermon-Lodève (1507-1538). They are found in most of the non-story windows.

13) Chapel of Our Lady of Pity

Retable in stone from the 17th century. The Pietrà, sitting on a throne in the arching above the altar, evokes the present title of this chapel. On the other hand, nothing reminds us of the former dedication of St James, Patron of pilgrims to Compostella.

WINDOW OF ARNAUD DE MOLES (n° 3)

General theme : an invitation to a spiritual rebirth, under the patronage of the Black Virgin.

In the mullions : Samuel et Heliah, in a heaven spangled with stars. *Characters at the foot* : Abraham and Melchisedek (pl. 10), St Paul the Apostle, the sibyl of Samos. At the bottom: the Sacrifice of Isaac, conversion of St Paul, Nativity of Jesus (pl. 12).

14) Chapel of St Anne

The altar and statue of St Anne are a modern set without artistic value.

On the east wall, a Gothic credence and door to the crypt.

WINDOW OF ARNAUD DE MOLES (n° 4, 5 and 6)

General theme : the crossing of the desert, a formidable trial. Emphasis is placed on the Word of God, a freeing word according to the ability to listen.

In the mullions : Heliah and the sibyl Persica; at a lower level: Mary, the Virgin Mother. *Characters at the foot* : Isaac, Samuel and Osiah. *At the bottom* : parts of a Renaissance interior, two medallions: Pierre de Beaujeu and Anne de Beaujeu.

N° 5. *Characters at the foot* : Jacob, Jonas, St Mark the Evangelist. *In the bottom part* : Jonas and the sea monster. At the right and left of this Renaissance portico, two symmetrical medallions : Jean V, last Count of Armagnac, murdered in 1473.

N° 6. *In the mullions* : the coat of arms of Beaujeu, above the Angel holding an ensign to the glory of Mary. *Characters at the foot* : Moses, the sibyl Libyca, Enoch. *At the bottom* : Moses and the Burning Bush (pl. 13), the sibyl and the Emperor Augustus, Enoch assumed into heaven.

15) Chapel of St Catherine

On the east wall, only since the 18th century, the door opened into the Archbishop's Chapel.

The altar and retable are of the 16th century, in Renaissance style. They date from 1524. In the niches, St Peter, St Catherine, St Henry. These three statues are recent.

In the upper part, dolphins meet or play with a child. It is the same them on the front of the altar. In a band, above the altar, eight Apostles are ordered around Christ.

This altar and retable are rich in many miniatures, in the manner of illuminations. In the frieze running over the three pilasters, at the level of the heads of the three big statues, we read from the left to the right an inscription bearing a supplication to Mary and the date of this altar. Over the whole length of the pilasters are pyramids of details in bas-relief in relation with the details of the choir stalls. The south transept door appears to be in the same style.

WINDOW OF ARNAUD DE MOLES (n° 7, 8 and 9)

General theme : the entry into the Promised Land. The elect are all those who have passed through the trial of the desert.

N° 7. *In the mullions* : promotion of the Patriarch Joseph. *Characters at the foot* : Joseph, St Andrew the Apostle, Joel. *At the bottom* : Joseph sold by his brothers.

N° 8. *In the mullions* : Angel musicians (pl. 11). *Characters at the foot* : Josuah, the sibyl Europe, Amos. *At the bottom* : the flight into Egypt.

N° 9. *In the mullions* : the Holy Women : Saints Mary Magdalene, Catherine, Agatha, Lucy, Barbe. *Characters at the foot* : Caleb, St Bartholomew the Apostle, Abdias. *At the bottom* : the suffering of St Bartholomew.

In the band running through the three windows, above the characters at the foot, the symbolic history of Susanna, at the time of the Prophet Daniel, is evoked.

16) The Blessed Sacrament Chapel

Modern altar (1875) in gilded bronze. Behind, attached to the wall, is a statue of the Sacred Heart. Above is a baldachino in stone from the beginning of the 16th century. The fine ensemble of architecture, with its imitations of vault keystones, appears as a replica of the apse of a church, with a finely worked ceiling and everything in lace. On the imitations of vault keystones are five carvings: Christ teaching the four Evangelists. On the front part of the baldachino, at the middle, is a reminder of the dedication of this chapel: a carved chalice with the Host shown over it.

The painted "tapestries", from the end of the 19th century, are meant to harmonise the walls and the baldachino with the guided bronze of the altar. Four coats of arms (two Popes' arms and two Episcopal coats of arms) and two portraits are drawn. For the portraits: *to the right*, St Margaret Mary Alacoque (1647-1690), Visitation nun at Paray-le-Monial who spread devotion to the Sacred Heart ; *to the left*, St Francis de Sales (1567-1622), founder of the Order of the Visitation and a great mystic. Among others is one of his thoughts: "The most cowardly of all temptations is that if discouragement".

General theme : the Crucifixion, the Cross of Jesus. Several reactions are possible in its presence: scandal to the point of rejection, or trusting acceptance. In the mullions are the three fleurs de lys on a starred blue background, an evocation of the Royal arms.

N° 10. Isaiah, St Philip the Apostle, Micah.

N° 11. In the foreground of a profound and harmonious perspective, Jesus on the Cross. Mary, His Mother, St John the Apostle and St Mary Magdalene keep him company (pl. 7). This Crucifixion is situated in a golden rectangle, or in two superimposed squares. The square is the symbol of stability. A strong interior stability is found in the three looks turned to the Crucified Divine One.

N° 12. David, St James the Apostle the Greater, in the costume of a pilgrim to Compostella, Azarias.

17) Chapel of the Holy Sepulchre

In 1720, it bore the title of "royal chapel". It is on this site that the foundation stone of the Cathedral was laid on 4th July 1489. It was given the title of the Trinity, coming without doubt from the sculpture representing this mystery, in the top of the retable. The Confraternity of Merchants were accustomed to meeting there on the day of this Feast.

On the south wall, a Gothic credence. This chapel that adjoined the bishop's curia, never had a stained glass window. This lack is compensated by the incontestable interest of the Burial of Christ it contains. This monument is inspired by the mystery plays of the Middle Ages.

Our Burial of Christ (pl; 5) gathers the eight traditional characters : Jesus, the mother of Jesus, two other Maries, St John the Apostle, Mary Magdalene, finally, Joseph of Arimathea and Nicodemus who hold the shroud. The general expression appears as rigid as death; but we notice a confident serenity. This contemplation contrasts with the strange indifference of four isolated guards.

This Burial of Christ, in a way included in the set of our Renaissance windows after the crucifixion of Jesus, is certainly marked by the open-mindedness of this period. We find an underlying "screenplay" evoking the precise events and the concrete historic characters. A relational world, the one either lived or known by the various patrons, probably the same as those of our windows.

Each character is the one who is more or less centred by his attitude, details of costume, place, or the object held in his hand. And Mary, with a crown of thorns, appears us in a more particular light. She occupies even the central place, therefore a honour also noticed in her costume.

This group is like a family, with looks, and especially with their hearts turned toward the face of the dead Jesus, borne on a shroud. These are attitudes and feelings we find in all family gathering, at the time of a death. But, there, one would not be planning a funerary monument like our Burial of Christ. However, there are similarities. I think, among others, of the church of Brou, in the Ain, with its three truly sumptuous tombs in the sanctuary ; a church considered as a temple of fidelity, designed and constructed during this same period. It is a monument in which we find the regard and especially the heart of Margaret of Austria, the inspirer of this work.

This masterpiece, achieved toward 1500, would be owed, we think, to the chisel of Arnaud of Moles himself, or inspired of one of his working drawing. But, it is not certain that he had this adaptability, as the master glazier; like Leonardo da Vinci for example. The gilding, covering the bottom of the wall, dates from 1964, that of the canopy is older.

The canopy, of flamboyant style, is decorated with an original Trinity. It is the "showing" of Christ on the Cross, by God the Father himself. The Holy Spirit, symbolised by a dove, is placed between the Father and. the Son. This theophany is truly in relation with the Burial of Christ, and even more with the theological basis of the Passion, but not with the text properly said to be of the Gospels.

18) Chapel of Saint Louis

Before the Revolution, this chapel was a mere passage towards the sacristy. The altar retable is due to the sculptor Griffoul-Duval from Toulouse and to Lodoyer, city architect of Auch. The foundation stone was laid, in 1815, by the Duke of Angoulême in person. Among the Corinthian columns, we notice two bas-reliefs. The one of the bottom evokes the passage of the Jordan through the Ark of the Testament. The one at the top takes the same theme, in the history of Auch. They are a testimony of gratitude, a vow of our city, addressed to the Virgin Mary and St Louis, in gratitude for the protection granted to the French Crown, during the torments of the Revolution.

WINDOW OF ARNAUD DE MOLES (n° 13, 14 and 15)

General theme : the trial of the exile, that resembles a "burial". In the crucible of this suffering, a new "exodus" is prepared in the believer's heart.

N° 13 : Jeremiah, the sibyl Agrippa, Nahum. *At the bottom* : the flagellation of Christ.

N° 14 : Daniel, the sibyl Cimmerienna, St Matthew the Apostle. In *the bottom part* : Daniel in the lions' den.

N° 15 : Sophoniah, Elijah, Uriah. *To the bottom* : Elijah assumed into heaven.

At the south wall, the door opens into the sacristy ; the western door gives deal access to the crypt.

The crypt

The truth is that it is a false crypt. Indeed, it is not excavated, but rises on a foundation of rock. It was designed to support the end part of this Cathedral that was to be bigger than the others. From this, it is at the same level as the ground outside, as the small windows open onto the gardens of the old Archdiocesan curia, by a door that gave access from the cloisters of the canons' house.

The crypt includes five chapels, corresponding with to the luminous chapels of the apse. They have no decoration. The vaults, in Gothic style, are flattened. Relics and sarcophaguses of Saints of the diocese were put there. Besides, each of these chapels is dedicated to one or another among them: St Leothade, St Taurin, St Austinde, St Amand, St Clair,.

The sarcophagus of St Leothade deserves particular attention (pl. 17). It comes from the old Benedictine abbey of St Orens of Auch. Situated in the northernmost crypt chapel, it dates of the 7th century. It is a realisation of the school of Aquitaine. Finely worked, it is composed of a flared vat and a roof-like lid. Among the interlacing and vine branches, we see, on the vat and the lid, a very curious chrism, where the alpha and the omega are inverted.

This crypt was for a very long time a place of pilgrimage. They came to recollect themselves and pray before the reliquaries of the Saints. Two doors gave access there, from the apse of the Cathedral. Next to the accustomed, there were all the occasional pilgrims, especially those on their way to Compostella. They were very numerous until the 18th century.

The crypt contains tombs of Archbishops François Delemare, who died in 1871, Émile Énard, who died in 1907, Pierre of Langalerie (1871-1886) and of a prefect of the Gers Department Antoine of Lafitte, count of Montagut, who died in 1815.

The treasure : a date, perspectives.

Opposite the door of the entrance to the stalls, on the south side, there is a former sacristy, where various objects were stored, mainly liturgical. Works of the 15th and 16th centuries, most from the 18th and 19th. The initiative is due to the Beaux Arts, in May 1970, at the time of the Archaeological Convention of France.

On the east wall is, in a recess, were placed two statues : Henri of Albret and Margaret de Valois. They were married in 1527. Their visit to our Cathedral was in this same year. The two statues perpetuate this event. Margaret was the sister of François I, King of France.

Presently, the Beaux Arts see bigger. This is why, at the end of 1996, these various objects have been stored elsewhere for the meantime.

They will join others, in a vaster site, which is to be the crypt of our Cathedral, with an entrance from the Place Salinis. But before this is possible, there is some absolutely necessary work to do, among others in view to damp proofing.

19) Chapel of the Compassion

This chapel had been placed under the dedication of the Resurrection, then it received that of the Passion.

The various elements of its decor form an exceptional whole, remarkable by its unity and inspiration. There is a retable with its Virgin of Mercy, and 9 panels sculpted on woodwork covering the walls. The set of bas-reliefs, in gilded wood, evokes the main moments of Christ's Passion; successively, Jesus at the garden of Gethsemani, the kiss of Judas, Jesus before the High Priest, the flagellation, the crowning of thorns, the carrying of the Cross, the Crucifixion, Jesus on the Cross, brought down from the Cross. The canopy, overhanging the altar, presents the instruments of the Passion.

The retable of this chapel would have been installed by Jean Douillé himself towards 1662. As for the accompanying bas-reliefs, they seem to date from the same period, but appear to be made by someone else. They are marked by the tragic expression of the Spanish school. On the high border of the panels, monograms in bas-relief are to the honour of Mary and inspired by the Ave Maria.

WINDOW OF ARNAUD DE MOLES (n° 16)

General theme : the return from the Exile. God's hand proved to be decisive. In thanksgiving a whole people rebuilt the Temple.

In the mullions of this stained glass window and the next one, medallions of religious or political characters, who were the *initiators and founders,* or protectors of this Cathedral. *To the top* : arms of Cardinal de Lescun (1463-1483). *Lower,* at the level of angels who hold a cartel : Louis XII, King of France and the Milanese. *Characters at the bottom* : St Matthias the Apostle, Esdras, Habakuk, the sibyl of Tibur.

20) Chapel of Our Lady of Hope

Before 1825, this chapel was dedicated to the Ascension.

Retable in stone, of the 19th century. At the bottom, a painting evokes the Ascension. In the niche at the top, we see Our Lady of Hope.

At the south wall, a Gothic credence.

WINDOW OF ARNAUD DE MOLES (n° 17)

General theme : the Resurrection is presented like a transfiguration which is not won without effort or pain.

In the mullions : arms of the Cardinal of Savoy (on the right), 1483-1490, of the city of Auch (to the centre), of Cardinal of La Trémouille (on the left), 1490-1507 (cover. p. 4). *Characters at the bottom* : Elise, St Jude the Apostle, holding the saw of St Simon the Apostle, the sibyl of Delphes, Aggea. *In the bottom part,* Elise heals Naaman, martyrdom of the Apostle St James the Lesser, the crowning with thorns (pl. 14), arms of Clermont-Lodève (1507-1538).

21) Chapel of Our Lady

Previously dedicated to the Holy Spirit, this chapel is now dedicated to Our Lady since 1860. The retable has been raised with elements of the old choir screen that adjoined the west part of the stalls, in the transept crossing.

At the South wall, a Gothic credence and an inscription on a plate commemorating the restoration of this window, by Hirsch, in 1875.

On the floor, tomb and recumbent figure of Mgr de Salinis (1856-1861). This monument is the work of Michel Pascal (1861).

WINDOW OF ARNAUD DE MOLES (n° 18)

General theme : Resurrection of Jesus, both a summit and a path. It is especially a welcoming, always offered, according to the three apparitions represented here.

Characters at the bottom : St Thomas the Apostle, Christ, Marie Magdalene (pl. 8). *Lower* : in an intermediate frieze that runs over the whole width of the window: the date of this work (1513) and the artist's homage. *In the bottom part* : disciples of Emmaus and, on the right cartel, the name of Arnaud of Moles.

continued on p. 65

PLATES

CHOIR STALLS

21

28

30

31

IN CONCLUSION : HOMAGE AND RECOMMENDATIONS

Two cartels appear at the left and right of the lower part of this window, representing the apparition of Christ to the disciples of Emmaus. Their cords, of green emerald and a quick red, are held between the teeth of a character with a very expressive face. This face seems to be that of Arnaud de Moles.

On the right cartel, in the invitation addressed to Thomas in these terms: "Place your finger here", we find the proposition made to our master glazier. Therefore, we find confidence in his eye, his fingers and hands. A confidence in spite of everything, for our artist was of advanced age. His eyes were tired, after his years of effort for the various masterpieces with a multitude of details coming from his hands. His eyesight was poor, like that of Thomas. He had, himself, the equivalence of a risen Christ, his companion glaziers among other, also very qualified, and of course the various patrons.

But this whole, with the numerous plates of glass of which it consists, remains very fragile. This is why Arnaud de Moles seems to ask us very expressly, in the cartel of left: "Do not touch me!" From then on, it is as if he personified himself in his work. A fragility indeed! To compensate, a protective metal grating has been placed outside each window.

However, despite everything, restorations became necessary, that achieved by Hirsch in 1875 among others, for this window of the Resurrection. The reorganisation of the chapel with its new dedication had been the right occasion. Down below, on the wall, a marble plate brings us the memory, saying like an excuse: "Cautissime tangens". This means "We have had to touch this window, but it is with great care that we have done it".

In the set of the 18 windows, a whole spiritual journey comes to its end, with various calls, especially that addressed to Thomas: "Put your finger here!" Therefore, it is the equivalent of a "Take ye all and eat", that of the Holy Supper. However, it is necessary listen and be there.

Now, on the left cartel in the "Noli me tangere", it seems to us to read "Tacere". It is as if the Risen Christ asked us: "Do not reduce me to silence. Permit me to speak, because I have much to say". This lesson is for all times! Besides, in the central part of the window, Jesus looks towards St Mary Magdalene and those passing by. He has always been there.

THE CHOIR AND STALLS

The choir - Situation and definition

The choir seems like another church in the Cathedral. It is totally enclosed: at the east by the monumental retable of Pierre Souffron II; on the three other sides by the high stall canopies. Thus, it gives the impression of a secluded place, like a kind of symbolic desert. Besides, it was perfectly suited to the primary function of a choir: the place for the Capitular Office (p1.25). The monks and canons met there at certain hours of the day to fulfil the duty of their Office. The word: choir evokes singing and dialogue. The prayer of the canons was all these things at the same time. The many biblical themes represented on this woodwork, far from distracting them, brought them without cease into an atmosphere of prayer (pl. 23).

Stalls - Variety of details - Inspiration

The choir is above all the stalls (pl. 19). There are 113 of them. They are in wood, in heart of oak. This wood had first remained immersed for a long time in water. It could then be worked very finely, nearly in lacework. What first of all strikes the attentive mind is the wealth and the variety of details (pl. 26). Indeed, if we review the various elements of these stalls: the misericords, armrests, partitions and noses; the high canopies, backrests and pilasters; the canopy, passages and arching, we count no less that 1,500, all different. The source of this inspiration is not unique. Of course, the imagination and faith of the artist drew very extensively from the Bible and the live of the Saints. But nature was just as much an incomparable treasure: animals as much as plants. Mythology was also used. We also notices the presence of a crowd of monsters based on both man and beast (p1.29). They compare with details borrowed from pagan religions. One encounter themes of the Grail and chivalry. It is therefore a perfect coexistence and a happy harmony between two cultures, between two modes of thought, meeting each other: the mystical fervour of the Middle Ages and the very welcoming humanism of the Renaissance.

Authors and dates

The decor of stalls, which is Renaissance in many places, is located in a flamboyant Gothic architectural setting. Alas! We are unaware of everything about the authors of this remarkable masterpiece. This work remained indeed anonymous. The few inscriptions we find, here and there, teach us nothing about the personal identity of the artists. They only clarify the profound inspiration of the work. Who were they? From where did they come? According to a tradition, the artists would be none other that companion sculptors, the compagnons du devoir de liberté. With the humanism of the Renaissance, the compagnonnage worked in its own way. Some wanted themselves to be of the "duty of freedom". A very fine ideal! It also runs, like a message, over the whole length of the biblical narrative, in the stalls.

These companions have been able to give full initiative to their art, to the point of expressing in many places their school initiation, of course discreetly. But, anyway, they had to serve very faithfully the biblical theme that was proposed them. They did this conscientiously and with great intelligence (cover p.1).

However, concerning the artists, we know at least a name: Dominique Bertin. This sculptor from Toulouse was charged with some modifications or refitting, esteemed necessary, notably the transfer of presidency stalls to where they are located today. It was in 1552-1554. We have therefore established the finishing date. On the other hand, we are ignorant about the first beginnings. It is habitually admitted that this important work was begun in 1510-1520. From then on, work would have taken about forty years.

Message and alternations

However, this remarkable set is not mere art! It bears thought, containing a message (p1.33). The great originality of the stalls resides in this, in relation with most others. A story is told there. It is especially developed in the high canopies, as we advance, while respecting the intended order, since Adam and Eve, the high canopy of the Count's stall, up to the Holy Apostles Peter and Paul, above the Archbishop's stall. A story is told, in 69 pages, in as many canopies. In the high stalls, it is the life of the Hebrews that is evoked. On the other hand, in the low stalls, the pictures of various passages recall exclusively the essential events of the life of Jesus (pl. 21). We discover them as we following a parallel course, as progressive, from the Annunciation to the Crucifixion.

This harmony of thought is not obvious to first view, from the first. It has to be discovered. On the other hand, there is another ordering that is immediately noticed. It is an obvious alternation of masculine and feminine characters. They seem to advance, as in a solemn procession, two by two. Most the time this repeated alternation of two characters includes a man and a woman. It would be better to say a woman and a man. As soon as the first stall is passed, it is the woman who now takes the first place. This higher place seems a choice of courtesy, giving right to a moral priority.

Indeed, as soon as the ascent toward the altar is finished, when we return towards the Archbishop's stall of archbishop to conclude the cycle, then the order changes suddenly in the setting of the successive alternations. The order changes in the sense that the feminine characters find themselves facing the altar, or in a more comfortable and higher situation; for example, like the Virgin Mary herself, presiding and facing the altar, between the Archbishop's stall and that reserved for the Armagnacs.

Tragic aspect

On the other hand, when we carefully observe the details, in the stalls, something else immediately appears to our eyes. Demons and snakes, malevolent animals and monsters of all species swarm there (pl. 31). This invasion contributes to give to this whole a tragic aspect that also agrees very well with the profound movement of history that is narrated to us, as much in the high stalls as in the low stalls. This tragedy appears a deliberate desire, to such a point that, during the progress of the history of Jesus, we neglect to emphasise, in the reality of the sculptures, the very important fact of the Resurrection. On the other hand, the suffering and the torment of the painful Passion are developed extensively (pl. 22). Finally, this impression is only apparent, because it does not truly correspond with the most profound reality marked by a proven optimism (pl. 27).

But, anyway, this tragic aspect of our stalls is only a complementary aspect, that has to be put into relation with the parallel impression coming from the windows of Arnaud de Moles, appearing more optimistic. Finally, windows and stalls constitute a whole, very instructive, of which each element is as indispensable as the other, for the balance of thought is the perfection of art. Besides, these two masterpieces were designed at the same time. A same story is told. Its theme was proposed to the master glazier and to the sculptors. Feelings expressed, in a different manner if not opposed, practically evoke a same reality: the reality of man in general, the profound reality of the believer. The windows of Arnaud de Moles seem to us peaceful, more confident. Optimism and peace shine forth on every occasion, by the colour, the decor and drawing. They constitute the face of a man. They show us what appears in the life of a human being, under the burst of a resplendent sun. Stalls evoke the night, darkness and shade, the all the feelings these eternal symbols suggest. Our stalls are indeed far from light, far from the sky. They are the choir for prayer; they are yet the heart of a man. The heart of a man? That is to say the demons who live him, pangs and confrontations rendering him asunder (pl. 24), combats and choices bruising him in the measure that he commits himself.

The theme of life

One would almost think about Dante's Inferno. But, this obvious tragedy is not a hell. It is a path toward Life, toward success. Indeed, an unshakeable hope does not cease to bring this crowd of characters living in these stalls: characters that are all famous (pl. 20), whether they are Patriarchs and Prophets, or yet Apostles, Virtues and Holy Women of the Bible. They walk right before them, sustained by one same hope, like this very fine Charity (stall 2) going alone, but courageous, to face evil, the malevolent snake. She leaves empty handed. But, at the end of the cycle, she became the triumphant Strength (stall 66). Then, her mission is complete. She deserves a just promotion indeed (pl. 32); because we see all malevolent snakes crushed under her feet or finally mastered in her hands.

The theme of the Feast

From then on, the feast can be organised (pl. 30) since Life has just triumphed over Death. To signify the feast, the artist represented joyful processions on the pedestal of this triumphal Strength (stall 66), where riders and soldiers advance, carrying trophies symbolising their victory. However, this feast is prepared, and it is even already celebrated, all along the cycle, since Adam and Eve (stall 1), to the final stall. The signal is given by the famous childish round, opening by a happy dance, the cycle of the life of Christ, above the panel of the Annunciation (stall 68). We see carriers of garlands (stalls 43 and 61) and Angel musicians (stalls 81). Indeed, in spite of the malevolent snake and dragons of all species, it is still the feast. Besides, since this History is told and relived in retrospect, our artists knew in advance that this dramatic adventure had to bring us to Life (pl. 28).

Sibyls and mythology

The Sibyls, who are "seers" of the pagan world, are also present in the crucible of this dramatic history, where a people's future is played, where the destiny of a life is decided. This is why they are there! Mythology saw them born and made them prosper, and now holds them company in this sacred universe, where Patriarchs and Prophets are with the Apostles and Saints. However, the sibyls do not speak. They are as quiet as the Synagogue. They are maids; and the object that they hold recalls simply a biblical memory, to understand better the language of the Prophet, committing himself better to straighten the course of history.

Concerning the details borrowed from mythology, these are not a concession to Paganism. No, only an opening to this new culture. The epics of Hercules, the power of pagan gods appears exceptional, of course. However, the believer, reading the Bible, understood that there is better and yet more exceptional. For him, Christ appears a "Super-Hercules". From then on, the presence of these heroes of Antiquity does not seem out of place in a church, among other sculptures. They were there like a decoration, like an illumination, better as a feature that is strongly marked, bringing out a truth, emphasising a character.

Auch, at the heart of the Renaissance

What breadth! What perspectives! It is in this thought that comes out of the woodwork of the choir of Auch. We cannot avoid being impressed indeed, to such a point that some connoisseurs are not afraid to compare the extraordinary biblical flights of stalls with the exceptional frescos painted by Michelangelo on the vault of the Sistine chapel in Rome. In both cases, it is a perfect expression of the best mind of the Renaissance, in the domain of the Christian faith.

Our masters of though were at Auch, perhaps! But, without doubt, their thought came from elsewhere. Indeed, at the end of the 15th century and in the beginning of the 16th, our city was especially privileged. This luck explains largely the stalls and windows of Arnaud of Moles. This is so because Cardinal Clermont-Lodève, Archbishop of Auch, was the nephew of Georges d'Amboise, the much listened-to minister of the King of France, Louis XII. Georges d'Amboise was chosen by the Pope of Rome as Legate to the King of France. On the other hand, Clermont-Lodève was himself appointed as Ambassador of the King of France to the Pope of Rome. And again, Louis d'Amboise, brother of Georges and the other uncle of Clermont-Lodève, had received the nearby Archdiocese of Albi in charge. By this happy combination of circumstances, Auch was of course in the heart of the King of France. However, especially, we were in Rome, at the crossroads of the Italian Renaissance. In return, the Italian Renaissance did not delay to enter the heart of our city, our Cathedral, the choir woodwork and the windows of Arnaud de Moles.

Importance of the high canopies

These stalls therefore contain a message. This thought is revealed to us by the very precise characters speaking to us. They express themselves in turn, alone, or with others in a whole (pl.18). They speak us by the fact of their existence and that of their occupying a given place, carrying a given object or taking a given attitude. From then on, if we want truly to penetrate their mystery, it is necessary first to try to live in their company. However, all these characters, apparently mute and without life, who are they? Canon Caneto attempted successfully this difficult identification at the beginning of the 19th century. We adopt this nomenclature in its whole. However, some personal observations, from iconographical details, brought us to change some names there, about ten in all. The characters of the high canopies are numbered according to the order of stalls. We will classify them in the setting of the biblical themes corresponding with the various stages of the history of the Hebrews.

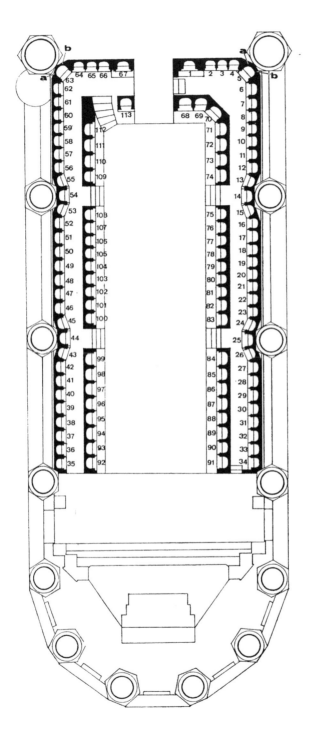

Plan of the stalls

ORDERING OF GREAT CHARACTERS

ABOVE THE DOOR OF THE CHOIR
St Jerome, the Virgin and Child, St Augustine,

IN THE HIGH CANOPIES OF THE STALLS

ORIGINAL SIN AND PROMISE OF GRACE
1   Adam and Eve
2   Charity
3   The Seer

TRIAL OF EGYPT, MOSES THE LIBERATOR
4   The sibyl Libyca
5a   Moses
5b   The sibyl of Samos
6   The Prophet Amos
7   The sibyl Persica
8   The Prophet Habakuk
9   The sibyl of Phrygia
10   The Prophet Malachy
11   The sibyl of Cumes
12   Saint John the Baptist

THE TIME AT SINAI AND THE NEW LAW
13   Religion
14   Saint Jean, the first disciple,
15   Hope
16   Saint Mark
17   Charity
18   Saint Matthew
19   Justice
20   Saint Luke
21   Patient Strength
22   Saint John
23   Mary Magdalene
24   Saint Peter
25   Martha and the tarasca
26   Noah

PROMISED EARTH, THE TIME OF THE JUDGES
27   Faith-Eucharist
28   Josuah
29   Jahel
30   The fleeting Sisata
31   Faith-Sacrifice
32   Jephtah
33   Abraham
34   Melchisedek

RETURN FROM THE EXILE? FINAL PROMOTION
67   The Apostles Peter and Paul
66   The triumphant Strength
65   The Prophet Zachariah
64   The sibyl of Erythrea
63b Calebs, lieutenant of Josuah,

TRIAL OF THE EXILE IN THE EMPIRE OF BABYLON
63a The sibyl Agrippa
62   The Prophet Isaiah
61   The sibyl Cimmeriana
60   The Prophet Aggeah
59   The sibyl of Tibur
58   The Prophet Daniel
57   The sibyl of Delphes
56   Jonas

FIDELITY AND INFIDELITY, FORTUNE AND INFORTUNE
55   The sibyl of Hellespont
54   The Centurion of Calvary
53   The sibyl Europe
52   The Prophet Jeremiah
51   The Dolorosa (or the Weeper)
50   The Prophet Ezekiel
49   Prudence (or Alliance)
48   Tobiah and his faithful dog
47   Judith decapitated Holopherne
46   Holopherne in pompous dress
45   Judith leaves for the mission
44   Holopherne as a soldier
43   Judith makes her choice

CLIMAX OF HISTORY, ROYALTY OF DAVID
42   David, with his trophies,
41   Jonathan, friend of David,
40   David with his frond
39   Goliath
38   David prepares for combat
37   Saul
36   Bethsabah
35   David, king,

ANOTHER STORY IN HISTORY

The 69 great characters of the choir and the 58 Renaissance windows are all, like each other, carriers of one history, that of the Bible. Their meaning does not stop there, at least for some of them. It is indeed a mystery that is beyond them, going largely beyond the biblical epic, to include the history of that time, that of the end of the 15th and the beginning of the 16th century, in France and even in the Europe of the period. This history is not told directly. It is implied, very discreetly written by fine touches under the cover of biblical characters. A detail in the costume, a particularly meaningful gesture, a resemblance on the face, or all other particularity, are as many signs, tracks, to introduce us to the heart of the other history. But, not just anyone can represent just anything. There must be a real concordance. And that supposes, to begin with, an obvious complicity between events or people, which one has decided to bring near to each other, to the point of sometimes making them coincide. Usually, this is not only one character, that is charged to carry the implication of a history, but a whole, his own, of which he is integral part, in the setting of a stained glass window for example. Thus, the various notes and other circumstantial details, brought by each, come to be added to those of all the others. It is therefore a whole that begins to shed light on the implied reality, so that it appears in daylight, with the best guarantee of certainty.

In his book, the De convivio, Dante spoke of this reading at several levels, when he evoked the four senses in any text: literal, allegorical, moral, spiritual. The allegorical sense is the one that corresponds to the other history. We can mention some names, evoked in the Cathedral of Auch: for France, Louis XI, Charles VIII, Louis XII, Anne of Beaujeu, Anne of Brittany, Louise of Savoie, the marriage of the dauphin François with Claude of France, Jean Marre and yet of others again. Representing foreign countries are Maximilian of Austria, Margaret of Austria, Pope Jules II, etc. But, not everything is there, of course. It is still hidden history, which, to be discovered, awaits shrewd eyes and an acute intelligence.

Why is this history evoked in our Cathedral of Auch? This question probably brings us until the patronage, and therefore to the heart of our Gascony, which was in political development at that time. The last Count of Armagnac, Jean V, died in 1473. This whole territory ever since found itself under the direct administration of the Crown of France. It is only in 1589, a the accession of King Henri IV, that Gascony became a part of France.

THE CHOIR RETABLE

Description and style

The retable that closes the choir at the east dates from the 17th century. It is due to the sculptor of Auch Pierre Souffron II, who undertook this monumental work from 1609.

It is in classical style, very influenced by Italian mannerism. On a base of stone, decorated with fluted pilasters, 22 columns or small columns of marble are ordered themselves, in front, between which are niches. Two pulpits are part of that whole: half way up, to the right and left. They are used at liturgical services for the readings and preaching. Spiral staircases inside the retable give access to the vast platform crowning the whole. Since 1860, the main sculptures of the old choir screen are placed on this gallery: 4 separated statues (Mary, St John, David and Isaiah) and the group of the four Evangelists. The two kettledrums are a memory, left by the Burgundy Knighthood regiment that had stayed a long time at Auch. They left them of it, together with their standards, at Christmas of 1776.

This retable joins the two ends of the woodwork, and so the choir is completely closed. Two doors, opening in these two prolongations, gave the canons access to the choir. Inside, two steles of marble are fixed on the stone above these two doors. We read there, in Latin, the enumeration of the Commandments of God and the Church.

However, this whole is not truly a retable to the strict meaning of the word. Indeed, it does not form a single unit with the altar, far from it. It was constructed for the purpose of the cause, to enclose the choir. On the other hand, this monument of architecture appears us excessively loaded, very complex in its composition.

A long-term project

The monumental choir retable was a long-term enterprise. Begun in 1609, it was achieved for the essential, in the years immediately following. This was notably the case for the closing wall between the pillars of the semi-circle as for the vast platform crowning the whole. The closing wall is presented on the side of the ambulatory like a two-story architectural composition. At each storey, cylindrical and fluted columns of Ionic or Corinthian order frame the doors that were originally apparently hidden. At the second storey, in the setting of the doors, stone bas-reliefs evoke the events of the life of the Holy Virgin. Only two have been realised: the Annunciation and the Visitation.

Other details

At the middle of the retable, a large portico in the arch opens onto a small chapel including an altar attached to the wall and, overhanging, a statue of the Virgin Mother, in white marble. For the liturgical needs in the choir, another altar, more massive, was installed, in front of the retable. It was adapted in 1860, at the time of the laying of the mosaic.

The small chapel behind calls permanently for a double memory. It is indeed in this same place that was situated, successively, the high altar, and of the first oratory built on the hill, and of Saint-Austinde's Cathedral.

The statue of the Virgin Mother, with the Child on her arm, took the place of two other statues since disappeared. The initiative was of the Constitutional Bishop Barthe. One, in wood, dominated the choir. In times of great calamity, it was brought down and made accessible to the public. It was burnt during the Revolution. The other, in silver, a Virgin Mother seated with her Child on her knees, remained in a fixed place. This also disappeared during the Revolution. There remains an evocation, in bas-relief, on the front part of the high altar. And the monogram, AM (Ave Maria), on the mosaic at the foot of the altar, is a supplication to her.

The dedication of the Cathedral, which is none other than the Nativity of Mary, is represented in bas-relief on the retable itself, over of the portico in the arch. We find evoked, in detail, the first washing and care of the young baby, Mary, carried by her mother Anne. The mother is still lying down, and God the Father dominates this scene.

In the niches of the retable, the place of the statues is occupied by reliquaries. Four of them are reserved to holy Bishops of Auch: St Austinde and St Léothade, St Orens and St Taurin. On the altar are placed 6 candlesticks and a cross in gilded bronze. They were used for the coronation of Charles X. This whole, a work of Choiselat, is a donation of Cardinal de Rohan, in 1828.

Lower, on the mosaic, some funerary inscriptions showing the tombs of three Archbishops of Auch: Leonardo de Trapes who died in 1629, Antoine of Morlhon, who died in 1828, Cardinal Isoard who died in 1839.

The mosaic of the choir was only laid in about 1860, at the occasion of the arrangement of the "front choir", in the transept crossing. It rests on the old stone paving. In one of the corners, at the bottom left, two swastika type crosses are drawn on the mosaic.

THE GRAND ORGAN OF JEAN DE JOYEUSE

Construction

The grand organ of the Cathedral of Auch (pl. 15), counted among the finest of France, is installed on a vast gallery, at the west end of the central nave aisle.

Its construction is owed to a famous organ builder of the 17th century : Jean de Joyeuse, born around 1635 and died in 1698. Through him, Parisian organ building penetrated into the south of France. However, the initiative was that of Mgr de la Baume de Suze and the chapter, who wanted to complete the furnishing of the Cathedral with a grand organ that "would rival the most sumptuous instruments of the kingdom". In 1688, Joyeuse won Auch. He built the case in chestnut and the pipes in fine tin "without any alloy in it". In 1694, the installation was perfectly finished.

The monumental case of the organ is to be admired for its architectural proportions and fine sculptures: two big panels represent David, the king musician, and St Cecilia (pl. 16). Two caryatids support the towers of the big front pipes, surmounted by two eagles and two Angels. At the middle, Our Lady, a sceptre in her hand, is framed on both sides by Angel musicians. Above the organ, the rose window of the 17th century gives a beautiful effect, especially in the rays of the setting sun.

The instrument is the very type of the classical organ of the 17th century. Its stops are not characterised by power as in Romantic organs, but by clarity, the wealth of harmonics (tierce stop) and the stunning reeds (clarinet, tuba and trumpets). The French music of the 16th and 17th centuries "sounds" admirably on this instrument.

Restorations

In 1954, a first restoration was carried out encouraged by the musicologist Norbert Dufourq and the organ builder Victor Gonzalez. The instrument was saved from serious decrepitude.

In 1996, the Monuments Historiques undertook a second restoration entrusted to the organ builder Jean-François Muno who gave the brilliance and authentic sounds of the 17th century back to this organ.

THE ORGAN ON THE CHOIR SCREEN

From an instrumental point of view, the Cathedral of Auch has the advantage of possessing two organs, witnesses of two privileged and complementary periods, one of the classical period, an opus of Jean de Joyeuse and the second signed by Aristide Cavaillé-Coll, of the romantic period.

This last, of the 19th century, stands in the centre of the Cathedral, in the transept crossing, where it crowns the monumental choir screen standing against the west ends of the choir stalls.

Given by the Emperor Napoleon III and Empress Eugénie , it appears enclosed in a rich case in gilded wood, with Cordoba leather. Its architecture fits in elegantly in the vast decor that replaced the old choir screen.

The project and estimate of this instrument were approved in 1856. It has 2 manuals and 15 stops. Some of these stops are characteristic of the French Romantic period, for example the gambas, harmonic and octavianting flutes, the violas, the voix célestes and vox humana, the cor anglais.

Two presences still of our own time

These two organs bear the mark of a period, their own period to each one, in artistic terms, thought, sensitivity. A presence is materialised in their various details, some visible, most are more discreet, but expressed very strongly under the fingers of an organist to whom it is entrusted.

This is the case for liturgical celebrations, some very festive, or yet at a recital, or at our grand summer musical festival at Auch, in June. It is an occasion for a big dialogue, as much from the instrument itself and the organist, as for the numerous attentive listeners.

Traduction by Alizé Euro

IN CONCLUSION

At the end of this visit that was at times a pilgrimage, in the most mystical meaning of the word, we cannot neglect to pay homage to all those that built our Cathedral,and that made it so rich, so beautiful. Our homage is addressed without reserve to all artists, very clever, for the most anonymous, such as the architects and masons, the sculptors in stone or wood, the glaziers and other decorators, without forgetting the writers and musical instrument makers who give their thought and music together in this extraordinary whole.

R A Y M O N D   M O N T A N É